FILM FAVORITES
FOR PIANO SOLO

ARRANGED BY MARK HAYES

T0105923

ISBN 978-1-5400-8585-6

Visit Hal Leonard Online at
www.halleonard.com

Contact us:
Hal Leonard
7777 West Bluemound Road
Milwaukee, WI 53213
Email: info@halleonard.com

In Europe, contact:
Hal Leonard Europe Limited
42 Wigmore Street
Marylebone, London, W1U 2RN
Email: info@halleonardeurope.com

In Australia, contact:
Hal Leonard Australia Pty. Ltd.
4 Lentara Court
Cheltenham, Victoria, 3192 Australia
Email: info@halleonard.com.au

for Keats Ellis

CLIMB EV'RY MOUNTAIN

from THE SOUND OF MUSIC

Lyrics by OSCAR HAMMERSTEIN II
Music by RICHARD RODGERS
Arranged by Mark Hayes

Somewhat faster (♩ = ca. 84)

Slower (♩ = ca. 76)

for Melody Stroth

GABRIEL'S OBOE
from the Motion Picture THE MISSION

Music by ENNIO MORRICONE
Arranged by Mark Hayes

Slowly, freely (♩ = ca. 63)

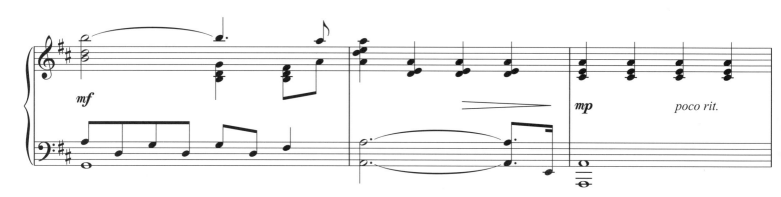

for Kathy Heine

THEME FROM "SCHINDLER'S LIST"

from the Universal Motion Picture SCHINDLER'S LIST

Music by JOHN WILLIAMS
Arranged by Mark Hayes

for Brad Handshy

GOD HELP THE OUTCASTS
from THE HUNCHBACK OF NOTRE DAME

Music by ALAN MENKEN
Lyrics by STEPHEN SCHWARTZ
Arranged by Mark Hayes

for Greg Gilpin

IF I ONLY HAD A BRAIN

from THE WIZARD OF OZ

Lyric by E.Y. "YIP" HARBURG
Music by HAROLD ARLEN
Arranged by Mark Hayes

for Joel Dumas

PART OF YOUR WORLD
from THE LITTLE MERMAID

Music by ALAN MENKEN
Lyrics by HOWARD ASHMAN
Arranged by Mark Hayes

for Jean Anne Shafferman

PEOPLE
from FUNNY GIRL

Words by BOB MERRIILL
Music by JULE STYNE
Arranged by Mark Hayes

Moderately, freely (♩ = ca. 84)

for Andy Waggoner

SINGIN' IN THE RAIN

from SINGIN' IN THE RAIN

Lyric by ARTHUR FREED
Music by NACIO HERB BROWN
Arranged by Mark Hayes

for Kayla Dowling

UNCHAINED MELODY
from the Motion Picture UNCHAINED

Lyric by HY ZARET
Music by ALEX NORTH
Arranged by Mark Hayes

for Jaclyn Beaulieu

SOMEWHERE, MY LOVE
Lara's Theme from DOCTOR ZHIVAGO

Lyric by PAUL FRANCIS WEBSTER
Music by MAURICE JARRE
Arranged by Mark Hayes